FINISHING LINE PRESS

www.finishinglinepress.com

Foraging for Light

poems by

Jan Zlotnik Schmidt

Finishing Line Press
Georgetown, Kentucky

Foraging for Light

Publisher: Leah Maines
Editor: Christen Kincaid
Cover Art: Dylan Todd
Author Photo: Philip A. Schmidt
Cover Design: Elizabeth Maines McCleavy

Printed in the USA on acid-free paper.
Order online: www.finishinglinepress.com
          also available on amazon.com

Author inquiries and mail orders:
Finishing Line Press
P. O. Box 1626
Georgetown, Kentucky 40324
U. S. A.

Table of Contents

Part IV

Part I

Vermeer's Lady Writing

She stares straight into our world
Her gaze penetrating centuries
A woman writing and waiting
Stories poised to be told
On her lips by her hand
Fingers arched
She scorns the world's gaze
She is not a scribbling woman

Another girl in another time
Signs her name over and over
In aquamarine ink that bleeds
And smudges on white lined pages
She writes her name again and again
In cursive Jan Toby Zlotnik Jan Toby Zlotnik
Loops on the y on the z…..her own flourish

The name precedes her thoughts
The words and worlds she imagines
At night in a blue and white room
A stream of a street light filtering through blinds
She writes in invisible ink
All the stories she won't tell anyone
All the words she swallows
All the screeches in her head

She imagines her thoughts
Like starlings crashing against glass
Against window panes in a storm

Sometimes she draws swans' arched necks
Curved beaks black eyes
Swans gliding across an undammed stream
In the quiet she draws into herself

The woman in ermine and a lemon gold frock
Gazes at her across the centuries

The crowds in the museum disappear
The woman's words not yet formed
The gesture half finished

The woman and the girl reach across time
In the stillness of their longing.

Icarus's Mother

When he fell through the sky
like a struck flare
his fingers almost touched sea and earth
then his body thinned to
scales of fish
watching the world

She imagined this
His arc of flight
his back bursting in flame
She unable to follow his course
to hear his words
seared
like burnt parchment

She learned to fear nothing

In another time
she saw the father
in his cell
watched him shape
elegant gold wings
of wax and feather

Watched them
magically take off
The boy eager to
touch the bright blue
edge of the world

Then the fall
against a vanishing sun

And now she bends
into herself
caught in her own labyrinth
her own grief and rage

And what she remembers
is a body alight
and glowing

Kentucky Hill Wife

She hears the blackbirds' incessant caw, goes to the front door. She remembers the scrape of his boots against the planked floor. Against the grain. Then the tight grip on her wrist. The whitened imprint of his fingers against blue veins. She clenches her fist. Now she's alone. He's left with the others. Gone to the creek to stop the water. Stop it from rising over the banks. Stop the currents from flooding the streets, the paths, the gulleys of her small town. Creek waters that would seep into the yard, the basement, the floors of the house perched too close to the mountains. She backs away from the threshold, the damp mold, the rot of stubbled corn, browned marigolds, tomato vines, skunk cabbage, creeping in with the morning air. The grass and weeds flattened like thin reeds. Flattened by mud. By the force of the river's course. There is a buzzing in her head, a blue static. She presses her fingers to her closed eyes. Presses coolness against her twitching lids. Waits for the static to turn to quiet. To a silence that will fill her body and stop her heart from pounding, Finally her breath slows. She turns to dishes, to cupboard, to open a cabinet door. There, on the inside wood with a stub of a pencil, she draws wings like Vs, then thick letters. The curves and loops of words, the swirl of them like a whirlwind in her mind. Letters curving around themselves, letters in short bursts, etched words that still the beating of her heart. Then she presses her name into wood. Writes it again and again. She knows he will not find her there. A stream of letters wavering across her sight.

Punta Mujeres: A Land of Grief

This is a land scorched
by fire, pumice, and flame,
charred lava rocks that lead down to the sea

This is a land where old women
shuffle slowly and look directly
Into cloudless skies

And they beckon to us
point to small green and purple figs
offerings wrinkled as they are

This is the land of old women
who mince their steps
mouth words through the gaps in their teeth

Their words betray no doubt
No shame in aging
or keening

They birth ten or twelve
Gather them in the folds of their dresses
 like lost letters

They know the power of tides
the tormentas, the calima
The power to destroy

And they walk in
their own shadows
forsaken angels.

Bess's Lament

I didn't know he was a magic man, a shape-shifter. When I met him, he was Erik, trapeze artist, diminuitive Jew. I knew he liked streudel, stuffed cabbage, his mother's babka. He held me with his bird fingers—cupping my chin— teasing me with his flashing eyes. I dreamt he was small enough to fit in my pocket. Fold him up in quarters like a white handkerchief, to keep him near.

In the beginning, I was his magic girl. Swish. I hear it still. The whoosh of the black cloth over the box. The swords chiseled in. Never touching my flesh. Stepping out, I smiled. Released from danger. Never scared. Never scarred.

Then he became Houdini. The only trace of our act together, the way he twined and untwined my curls at night. I had my own disappearing act. He dazzled, unlocked manacles, handcuffs, climbed out of milk cans, trunks, coffins. My upside-down man unleashed himself from a straitjacket in midair as I held my breath.

He called me his "gamin girl." And that was what I wanted. Always to keep a small flame for him, before and even after death. Do ghosts have breath?

In my old age, I became what I always was. A forsaken angel with wings of stone.

Io in Modern Dress

(About Lucien Freud's "Girl with a Leaf")

The spiked leaf pierces my eye. I was the one who couldn't close her eyes at night. The one who peered through the pane and saw silhouettes. Naked limbs strutting away from me. I was the one who saw shadows of bodies and tasted the salt and silt of dead seas

It was no different when he came to me, no different to see the body of a man who was a god. No different to be claimed by the razor edge of a glance. A piercing line of sight claiming by body my fate. The edge of the vine leaf sparks a sharp pain. A scratch against the white of my eye. My eye scarred, pulsed open by this forbidden view.

I couldn't help but see. Seeing so much like possession.

Now as he dresses himself away from me, I imagine his naked body, his white limbs. His back a sheen of muscle. His words a shimmer of rivers. His body a universe unto itself.

I say nothing.

I am tangled in vines, pricked and plundered.
My body turned foreign. Unknown to me.

All for a forbidden glance. My punishment for naked sight. I am my own plague.

Clara Peeters Speaks: Still Lives

(Active 1607-1621)

How foolish these men. They see garlic bulbs, bruised, lemons half- peeled.
Skeletal fish stripped of their flesh, tankards tipped, drained of ale.
They paint empty oyster shells, pomegranate seeds, bursting forth from
rotting skin.
I see spiked artichokes, leaves gloss green.
Grapes and cherries touched with sunlight. A warmth inside out.
Yes, fish die—slick on a plate, scales still wet with the sea.
Eyes glaring as if to say, "I know my place. My worth in your world."
Yes, the peregrine falcon stares at his kill: kingfisher, finch, a parrot.
A dread of colors. Yet for me lustrous celadon bowls
rest next to pink crab and crayfish. Clustered not devoured.
A hunk of Gouda, a pewter tankard. No hints of a dessicated world.
Just my bearing, my sight. My profile haunts.
Reflections in a goblet, in wreaths of silver on a decanter.
A trace of myself in a claret glass.*
I smile, place my signature P in twisted bread. Just a little secret.
His earthbound universe mine. This earthbound world unbound.

*Clara Peeters inserted self-portraits in her still life paintings. One of them had seven
hidden self-portraits.

Hopper's Women

"New York Theatre"

She would like to think she can
undo what has been done.

She would like to think the gilded cornices the ruby weave
the thick plush of the curtain presages a world.

She would like to think her breath
counts among the stars.

That her solitude means something
that her words have a point.

Black and white shadows course against her sight.
They hover against the tilt of the world.

"Cape Cod Couple at Twilight"

The yellow brown reeds
reach nowhere.
They shudder in a sea wind.

He smokes.
The white plumes evaporate in air.
A yellow orange flicker of ash,
a sign in twilight
like a falling star.

In the heat of summer
He will turn to her.
She knows this,
but she will have none of it.

At night, she dreams
she sees the yellow eyes of the fox
gleaming at her from

the depths of the forest.

The dog will no longer fetch.
He can't find the bone
In the high grasses.

The marsh will not give way.
There is no path to home.

"Morning Sun"

What does it take to be a muse?
Do you bring plush slippers?
A martini with three olives
on a stick?
Do you stroke a forehead
lick a cheek like an abject, hungry dog?

Do you arch your back
Feel the rose silk
rinse your body
in cool light and shadow?

Do your bones
your fingers your toes
stretch into the space
left by his presence?

You know you are worth more
than the angle of your chin
the tilt of your body
the strokes of the painter's brush.

You want to burn free
of the figure of the woman
resting on a bed.

A Ghazal: Not All White

(Response to Agnes Martin's White Paintings)

Not all white

Like the white blue tint of moonlight
on frozen lakes at night

Or the static of an almost
empty house at night

Paper whites and narcissus
unfolding at night

Blue lines on pure paper
The peal of an emptied mind at night.

Part II

I am a dutiful daughter

I am a dutiful daughter.
These words are carved on my flesh.

I will wash crusted sleepers
from your eyes,
clip the whiskers
on your chin.
Cool your skin
with rose water
in summer's heat.

And I will enter
the dark swamp
of your unwashed dreams.
Pull your
neck shoulders
torso toes
from the muck.

I will preserve
your quiet
like peaches
glistening in a jar
and smooth out the wrinkles
of knowing and unknowing
at your behest.

As your eyes
glaze into forgetfulness,
I will settle
next to your bones
your breath
your empty breasts
as your secrets
spill into my dreams.

Palette of Grief

The sea has its cycle of grief
Steel blue gray for the mourning mother
Electric blue for the bereaved spouse
Aquamarine for dreams without sorrow
Sea blue green for the temptation
to leave salt and tides behind
And streaks of purple for
the witnessing to come
The space in the heart
where joy was The memory
of it still a thrill in the bones
Deep satisfying indigo
seeping into ocean waters
edging toward the
violet line of the horizon.

Under Siege

You know why women on buses
rant, pull at their hair,
pick at their lips,
dig their nails into flesh.
You gaze at them longingly
You want that release.

"Fuck you.
Turn water into stone.
Fuck you.
They're in your houses
Your telephone lines
They're poisoning your food."

You wish you could
spit words like the
plagues at Passover.
"Boils. Vermin.
Frogs. Cattle Disease.
The slaying of the First Born."

The others on the bus
caution, "Hush shhh."
"She's one of the crazy ones."
"Maybe she'll stop."
They don't imagine
what you know.

Times when you could rip
clothes from your body
stream naked through
the streets at twilight.
Or chew on the skin between
thumb and second finger
until blood rises.

They don't know

fingers close around your throat.
You open your mouth
no words—only false hands
touching your body, your shame.
You remember.

Or you open your mouth
like a captive beast
and ropes burn your skin
pulling you in tighter.
Tighter.
You see dark thick burns
on your body
like swatches of rust.
You wish you still were alive.

You see your body
a hollow torso
spinning in space
falling limb by limb
until your bones splinter
as they hit the ground.

You watch
your body die
in water
in waves
in air
in fire
in flame.

You know what it means
to be a body besieged
dismembered
left rotting in woods
gnawed at by maggots
devoured by wolves.

"Bastards
Fuckers
They destroy
your heart."

You know her.
You just won't scream.

Do you hear my words as a whisper?

Do you hear my words as a whisper?
Hear them from far away
as if in a night wind?

Do you hear them as a calling
an echo or not at all?
Your lips clenched in a fit of anger.

All we once had were words,
stories to remember,
You, a young father, in a stiff back chair;
me, at bedtime, a little girl, chin up
to the edge of covers, listening.

And where are we now?
I press my fingers to your flannelled chest.
Your eyes shut against it all.
No syllables from your tongue.

Not a nod, a single word,
not Yes or No.
Just silence dead air
and your shuttered eyes.

How do I know you
now that words are gone?
How do I know the darkness
or light you live in?

A fluorescence
that turns flesh cold,
skin pale,
limbs weak.

I cast my line
into light-stained waters
of memory.

The Leopard Housecoat

During her last days my mother
shuffled from bed to bath
to kitchen table,
her feet scraping against
the cracked linoleum.

Step on a crack
Break your mother's back.
Step on a line
Break your father's spine.

A child, I stepped carefully over
the ruts and spider lines
in pavement, assured
my parents would live forever.
I would make it so.

In the evening she played
Scrabble on the kitchen table,
making nonsense words
nonsense syllables
as she straightened the round collar
of her leopard housecoat.

We played into the night.
She cuffed each sleeve, smoothed the creases,
cupped her hands in her lap
as she pondered the board.

We didn't correct her.
Then her words:
"Quiet.
The leopards are sleeping."

Twenty-Five Years After John Lennon's Death: December 8, 2005

Twenty-five years ago
in front of a classroom
in Richmond, Kentucky
I read aloud Dylan Thomas's
Child's Christmas in Wales.
My chest still damp
from my newborn's breath
from his suckling
still damp from
milk dotting my silk shirt
like thick flakes of melted snow.

I read quietly.
The words swirled in the room
like the first drifts
of a winter storm
weighing down pine and cypress
coating the circuitous paths
the woods and meadows
of the small Welsh town.

I imagined the children's
fingers and toes red with cold
their mouths open ready
 to catch the first flakes
their arms digging into drifts.
I saw blue hats
and red mufflers
like birds caught
in a frieze against the cold.

I chanted and entranced the class
felt all at once the cold
the snow and my son's presence
 his cheek against my chest
 his arms around my neck.

I imagined him
at two three and four
flat in a white meadow
arms brushing the snow
the imprint of wings against the sky.

Then as the milk started to flow
the door swung open
A student reeled in
"Killed." Gone."
Syllables wound down
into two iconic words.
The world stopped.

Now twenty-five years later
the world has stopped
so many times

and my red-haired son
the one with glowing blue eyes
has gone from me
into hollows of snow
I can't know.

And I am left
to imagine the places
where his body could fall.

This is a story about terrible itching.

I can't remember whether I sat on
a nest of red ants that crawled
into my underpants, into my privates,
and bit, small red stings that swelled
itched and burned from the inside out.
Or if it was my grandmother who sat on the nest
in the clearing on the side of the road
because she couldn't wait any longer to go.
She came screaming out from the woods,
pulling up her housedress,
her voluminous underwear caught
around her rubber stockings and her ankles....
Slapping at her crotch and thighs
like she was possessed by a demon,
she screamed in shock and pain. Then came the unbearable
itching, stinging like the burn of nettles,
small fires inside her flesh.

Or maybe it was a different time.
Maybe she crouched down on poison ivy,
thinking it was a patch of weeds,
 on the way to the Catskills, all of us in the car,
her figure merging into mine,
and then later her thighs were
covered in red blisters that oozed and burned.
Or maybe I had the chicken pox
and my blisters itched, crusted, and oozed.
I couldn't stop scratching...yearning for relief,
from the cooling oatmeal bath.

And was it my grandmother or me
who saw that itching that burning as a sign
of an assaulted body a body
that had to bear its scabbed flesh,
wounds of an alcoholic husband and
grandfather who clutched at our hands
as we tried to pull him up from the floor

since he was soused, semi-comatose.
This husband and grandpa who spat
yellow phlegm in the sink and drank
until he dropped in his gatkes
with absent yet glaring eyes.

Does it really matter
who sat on the ants
or patch of poison ivy
or whether she was going to the Catskills
or whether I was in camp at
Laurel Ridge and eight years old?
Memory burns. Pustules still ooze,
still raw still unhealed.

Madison, Wisconsin, May 1970 (After Kent State)

"Take off your thirsty boots
And stay for awhile
Your feet are hot and weary
From a dusty mile
 maybe I can make you laugh maybe I can try
I'm just looking for the evening the morning in your eyes."

Eric Andersen's "Thirsty Boots"

Take off your thirsty boots
and stay for a while this was what
the curly haired lover sang to her on a dusty mile
on a day when there were fires sirens
clouds of tear gas stinging their eyes.
On a day when they were armed with stones in their pockets
arms ready to fling rocks at the cops.

He saw her in the midst of
rubble yells and screams.
Pigs! Pigs! After gunshots
and fallen bodies
after napalm rain fell in places so far away
they couldn't fully imagine the burning
the scorched leaves in tropical forests
or the darkness in country.

Wearily, they held on to each other and stayed
for a while. He with his stout build
and wide arms that took her in
 her still young and muddy soul
yearning for a resting place.
Her blue velvet riding skirt flared in the sun
stuck to her skin in early morning.
Her grin replaced by aching need.

On a dusty stretch of country road
they shared secrets the pale yellow
green of the Plains stretching out before them.

They told each other stories and watched the sun set
stones still weighing down their pockets.
She remembers her hair in pig tails,
her denim overalls collapsing over her thin body
as she looked for the evening and morning in his eyes.

Then in the midst of dust and acrid smoke after
he gave her a damp handkerchief to cover her mouth
her nose so she wouldn't breathe in fumes of gas
after nights with sirens blaring and search lights
that framed the bedroom window
after they rested in the curves and warmth of their bodies
with their bloodied words and muddy selves
as the world reeled around he was gone.

Without a word. Gone.

Now the song returns.
The girl in pig tails and cowboy boots
is long gone and white stones
gathered at the edge of the shore
travel to grave sites and rest
with shards of mussels oysters clams
iridescent fragments in a bowl by her bed.

The girl treks through paths of memory
through a dusty mile
through present worlds littered
with shattered glass fallen bodies fires,
sirens and tears. She wanders through
the broken places in this world
searching for the shadow of herself in the ruins.
Looking at the evening the mourning in her eyes.

Part III

My Young Grandparents at a Coney Island Photo Booth circa 1900

She wants to be Houdini. Climb out of chains and rope, out of trunks, and crates, surge up to the surface of the air. Recover the world again. She wants to be a magician. Her body as light as snow falling softly on city streets. She wants. She wants to tighten cold metal links around her body, crawl in and out of jute and burlap, unknot herself. Break through a metallic cage.

She married the snake charmer with ice blue eyes, a diamond stick pin, and serge suit. Didn't see the leer in his smile. Didn't notice the bile in his thoughts. The jaundiced skin. The slim fingers that picked at wounds.

She wants to be Houdini. Or at least his wife. Watch his fingers in sleep knot and unknot twine. Watch his arms climb up and up imaginary ladders to the surface of the sea. She watches the wife wrap her husband in clinking chains. Sees the small slim man curl into himself into the dark of the crate. His wife draws a curtain; she disappears. Then he emerges, free, opens the crate, and she steps out, unscathed. Arms extended, smiling triumphantly at the audience.

They take the picture after the magic show. After the sea wind stung their eyes, their chafed lips, after they saw the fancy people at the grand hotels with sculpted paths bordering the sea, after she looked straight at the bathers, sun and sand. Nothing grand about the walkup on Smith Street with its smell of the pork and sausage store below. She thought of Barney the furrier who took her across the Brooklyn Bridge, promised her diamonds and a brownstone near Prospect Park.

But now it's the after time. Their faces poke through the openings in cardboard— its edge scraping her cheek. Her eyes chips of blue marble. His like ice. Their fake bodies droop, limp arms and legs. Dangling legs like rag dolls. In the photo she's in a black mourning dress; he's in a bathing costume. Between them is a little boy in a funereal pose. She doesn't know who he is. Staring at them is a crescent moon. And a man in the moon, a ghoul in the moon, glaring.

She waits for the picture to be taken. Then she can be released.

She wants to be Houdini's wife and take off the manacles that bind her. Rise to the surface of her dreams, gasping for breath.

My Parents as Young Lovers at Coney Island

Where did they come from, this couple? These two people whose bodies barely touched when I, their child, knew them. Here they are caught up in each other, in the heat of the moment. Are they really that happy or is it just a pose?

Behind them bathers splash in the white sea while oblivious to the scene, my parents lean against the railing of the boardwalk, not about to get their pristine clothes crusted with salt and sand. His chest puffed out, possessive, he wraps his arm around her shoulder, her white starched sailor blouse, cinched at the waist. In a blue blazer, white pants and white bucks, he looks quite dapper. My mother smiles, a white cap haloing her face; his eyes, catlike, hint at pleasures to come.

This is their beginning.

He will read her Keats and Shakespeare sonnets. He will woo her with his words, his earnest innocence, his quiet desire. Unschooled in mating, his poems will be his prop, his security. For she is the first one, the only one he ever loved. She will give in to him, to his seductions, as a poet. She will yield, a gesture so uncommon in her later years. They will court in twilight in Fort Greene Park, and he will read her passages from *Of Human Bondage*, his favorite novel. In him she will see a tableau for a larger life; he will see in her an escape from his mother's ranting, his father's harsh Russian words and bulk.

They bond. They are bound.

This is years before I was born, before the miscarriages, before his beloved younger sister died of cancer, before World War II and the atom bomb. Before disappointment halted their growth.

For the moment they are young, each holding on to their dream of the other. Fledgling spirits, warmed by an invisible sun.

Wedding Relic

A white gardenia on the lapel of her beige suit. A thick scent drifts over them like fog.

Her eyes are cat slits, her mouth pursed ready for a kiss. She sees no arthritic fingers, no swollen knees, no rubber stockings that she must pull up over her mother's stout legs, no cabbage and potatoes, no smell of urine from her father's night shirt, no house shared with relatives in Bayonne once her father lost the store, no handouts. She wants her body to be light, buoyed up by romance and his poetry.

He wants to leave behind a world of Russian immigrants, boiled chicken, chopped herring, kitchen walls lathered with grease, corners of rooms haunted by Yiddish and Russian syllables, so grating to the ear. He doesn't want to be weighed down by the spectre of a vast abandoned land. A past his parents never spoke of.

The only caption on the photo: Wedding 1935. No names—no Harold or Mae. Not yet.

They haven't named themselves, become who the other wills them to be. Later, in rooms blanketed by a fog of need, they will speak each other's names in the dark.

During World War II: Bakersfield, 1940s

They live with the thirst of knowing this was their beginning, this parched land in the desert.

They are anxious to please each other during the day or night. Their smiles are broad—her arm encircles his shoulder, he leans into her without that later stiffness, that starched spine, that stony glance that absorbed her sweetness.

They inhale desert air and watch butterflies drawn to the black brush turpentine plant. They learn that yucca, creosote and Joshua trees live for hundreds and hundreds of years. This gives them hope.

They grow their roots in this desert, take long walks on cool nights. He traces the patterns of stars: Andromeda, Ursa Major, Orion; she can't piece together the flickering lights into a pattern, but she pretends she sees all that he does.

They are far away from war, from bombings, from carnage, from their Brooklyn streets.

Later they will learn what gives the stars their blue tint—the vast emptiness of space.

My Mother Takes Aim: A Newlywed in the Desert of California

What was she aiming at? Rabbits? Prairie dogs? Tin cans? Her shoulder and forearm leaned into the butt of the rifle, her second finger ready to pull the trigger. Eye on the sight, she threw herself into the shot—her muscles fired up by the nearness of danger. Was my father in the background, urging her on? Was she posing as Annie Oakley? Did she take the shot? How do I mesh this image of my mother—pearl charm bracelet, spectator pumps, blue silk blouse and pleated skirt—with this smiling woman in overalls and oxfords? Was this her one reckless moment?

Behind her the blurred hills of the desert, the place where they escaped the war, where they roamed free of worry. Perhaps tin the spring the land was yellowed by wild dandelion, blued by lupine. A decade of wildflowers' offering of optimism.

Here, her life stood open before her. Then the return to a railroad flat on 55th Street. Miscarriages. Finally two children. Teaching. Bedding down with a husband working four jobs to satisfy her need for riches, yet controlling her with his silent withdrawal, squashing her atavistic desire for more. More of what—this was the mystery. I always was puzzled by her discontent. Did she remember the desert, wishing they still were there, still young, still unencumbered? What were her dreams? One day she told me she was a child of the Depression—she didn't have time to dream. She turned stolid, armored, tackling her world with endless lists and check marks for all she did. Her life as controlled, as ordered as her starched, hair-sprayed bouffant.

Later, regret cast its shadow, her staunch stance. She slept next to him at night, walked with him during the day. He inspired her bitter words. And she stared at her children with a yellow eye. Silenced them with her acerbic tongue. Took aim.

Fade Out/Fade In

A little boy's face, a child's lips, curly brown hair, a cap and knickers. He sits on a Shetland pony, fading patches of white on the horse's rump. I don't know whether he's living in the apartment on Atlantic Avenue near Pinchuk Paints or the house on Fort Hamilton Parkway. Once he told me that his mother put him on the trolley in front of the paint store, and he traveled alone to first grade. Down Flatbush almost to the river—the electric lines of the streetcar sparking in the sun. He never said if he was afraid or happy to be on an adventure. He never told me much more about his childhood.

I look at him—back stiff, eyes turned to an invisible observer. Why did these Russian immigrant parents take this picture? The father knew no English except the words he needed for business and signed his name with an X; the mother made borscht, shav and boiled chicken. Was it their hope that their boy would be a Tom Mix, a real American cowboy? With a half-smile or half grimace (it is hard to tell), he sits quietly, patiently, waiting. Anticipating his future in a new world. And always there was his silence.

But it's his eyes that let me know who he was—small, dark, piercing. Sad. These same eyes are mine. I am three, sitting on a stool, half facing an easel, paint brush in my hand, ready to dot the empty canvas with color. Half turned to the camera, I hear my parents' commands—smile—smile—but I don't want to. I wonder why they have me dressed in a flowered smock, ready to be an artist. Why are adults so foolish? I don't want to be the subject of the camera's eye. But I say nothing.

Now his lips are sealed—his eyes almost dissolving into his skull. He glances at me—not a flicker of recognition. Gingerly he picks up smashed pieces of white bread between his fingers, brings them to his mouth, slowly chews. I watch; I wonder. Words close up inside me too—and they burn my throat.

When I ask my younger sister about the photograph, she tells me it wasn't my father—it was his brother, our uncle Mike. She's not sure though. Not sure at all.

Part IV

Going Home

(Paint Lick, Kentucky)

The huge white steer at the fence
stares at me like a flabby Buddha
His rump and thigh muscles
bulging and I have
a sudden urge to stroke
the thick flap of his Adam's apple
What would his flesh be like
against my skin?

In the next field
three stallions gallop
they take off their sleek bodies
brown glistening in the sun
A yellow brown haze rises

I wonder
What it would be like
if I pressed my second finger down
against the thin places
between their eyes? Would they wince
or nuzzle against my skin?

The road winds toward home
Almond-shaped yellow green leaves
shimmer in the wind
like thin shards of glass
A knot tightens in my throat
I ask for words
to stop the aching
to tell me what the aching means

And I know
there once were words
 I often spoke them
in the quiet open spaces where
my flesh touched the world.

Portents

You tell me you want the soles of my feet to burn
and give me moments when burning is freezing

You tell me you want my body to be hunched
and instead you stretch my spine, an angle of fire

You tell me my fingers will become white leprous
but you keep my hands from turning black

You tell me you will forsake me
Leave me to the weight of salt and dead seas

Tell me you will wither my skin
Turn my bones to dust to ash

You tell me that dust is what bodies are made of
not air or spirit or flesh or words

You tell me that my flesh is a blue vessel for words
but leave me speechless

You tell me to rest a smooth round white
stone under my tongue

Hold it in the palm of my hand and know
there are signs only the wind understands.

A Gift: Kentucky Nursing Home—Many Years Ago

It was a quiet late afternoon in early winter, close to Christmas. She was there to hear their stories, give them back their pasts. The fluorescent lights in the room were dim, and the shadows of their bodies were etched on the lavatory's green walls. They circled her waiting, walkers aside, bodies hunched, gnarled fingers gripping their knees. There was a hush in the room.

Then their stories:

'I ate burgoo, squirrel, possum. My daddy shot woodchuck, duck, and made the stew.'

Another—"The sap from the maple was yellow, honey gold."

And then muttered words: "There were coconuts in the trees we picked. A vision of thick palm leaves amidst red bud and magnolia."

She took a breath. Nodded. Although used to dementia, she was startled. Resisted the urge to say

"Really."

Then an old man in denim overalls, straps loose on his shoulder bones, shuffled toward her, scratching his bearded chin.

"Here for you."

He opened his palm. In it a greasy barbecued pork chop.

"Here a gift."

She choked down laughter, looked down. Ashamed of her response.

"Oh thank you. Thanks so much."

"A Christmas gift for you."

He stretched out his hand, and she put the chop in her flannel- lined pocket, grease staining her black pants and thigh. She held on to it for the rest of the session. Afraid to break the spell. Not wanting to leave his world. The world she was a stranger in. After all Christmas was a time for miracles.

Or she was young then.

The earth was still

The earth was still, she said. She could see the yellow green of leaves,
the way light passed through them like shadows of wings.

The earth was still she said. Too still. The graves were dug. The soil
crumbling under her fingertips.

The earth was still. Vagrant wings may move. Geese may take flight against
the sky. A white heron may twitch. A wave may break. But the earth was a
sheen of white air and space. And she found her place in that quiet. In that still
air.

She wanted to speak and then be still.

And her whispers would echo like the rustling of an animal in the leaves.
A quiet like a hum of water. A quiet like the cries of the dead.

Broken Ghazal

There were no bright stars in the night
My father told me he saw dreams in clouds.
There was no moon in the night
My father told me he touched its rays.
There was no wind in the night
My father told me leaves stirred like whispers.
There was no rain in the night
My father told me rain was the keening of the planets.
And there was no night
On the day my father told me
He breathed in words like air.

*****

There were no constellations in the night
When my dog's shadow was a dark second self
There was no moonlight in the night when
The shadow hovered next to me.
There was no memory in the night
When shadow and stars merged
And a half moon a pastel- print in the half -lit sky
Led me back to my father's words that floated in the night.

Flash Forward: On the Way to Graciosa with my Husband

(On the way to the Fortunate Islands)*

I see it ahead of me
Memory unraveling like a skein of longing

The wind pushes my gray hair back
away from my face, strands plastered
against my cheeks, my chin, my throat

We have done this journey before
Gone to this place where treasures were lost
where treasures were found

This land of seven hills
Of buried gold doubloons
This place where Columbus stopped
On his way to unknown continents

We look ahead of us
for the first sign of land
for the first white stretch
of beach and crooked huts

The waves pound against the shore
The boat tilts into the wind
The tides carry us forward
We have been here before

Ashore we stop in an unremarkable place
A seafood restaurant windows
spotted with salt
Sand dotting plastic tablecloths

We eat grilled octopus and dorado
Dip crusty bread
into green vinegar sauce
Oil coating our fingers circling our lips

We smile in this place
without streets or landmarks
just wind swept paths
almost indiscernible
traces in this pebbled world

Memory unravels
We will travel to the Fortunate Islands
again and again
Our bodies will arch
against wave and wind

And we will look
for shadows of ourselves
Remembering in dark months
the indigo sea
anticipating the journey back.

*The Fortunate Islands are another name for the Canary Islands, and one of them, Graciosa, is the site of Robert Louis Stevenson's *Treasure Island*.

Pompeii

She wanders the empty streets, her feet, stumbling on the edges of the smooth round stones, her heels almost caught in the ruts in the road, engraved by wagon wheels from so many centuries ago.

She steps over a threshold, into the empty space of a house, the stones at the door almost curved to the concave places of the heart, to the murmurs of the flesh. She stands in this center of the earth waiting for the woman to bend over an amphora of water or wine, waiting for a soft white robe to press past her as the woman prepares a feast of squab.

What will be left when she is gone? Will they find a white translucent shell and say she was there? Will they find a baby picture of a curly haired auburn boy holding a sunburst daisy up in the air? His copper hair speckled with light. Will they say he must be hers? Will they find a strand of gray hair against a blue rumpled sheet, or the imprint of a body in a flattened well of a chair, open copies of books, torn pages, a chipped tooth in an egg cup, or a scratched drawing of a blue swirling lobster on a thin yellowed paper? Will they find a stray pearl or a thick maroon velvet ribbon? Stained underwear or perhaps a crumbled note amidst the ruins?

Will they discover the accusatory words drawn from memory or the terrible dreams of a girl who wakes up at night unable to breathe, lost in serpentine alleys of a medieval city by the sea, unable to hear the rush of water against stone, unable to find the street that leads to the harbor, the path that opens into a wash of blue light?

Or will they find nothing. Just the outlines of a house.

She is the center of an empty world, the brick and mortar foundations still intact. She hears the open-mouthed howls of the dead as lava and pumice and gases and stones fill the sky and fall like a thick sheet of flame, a rain of fire. In the quiet she hears their groans. She sees their bodies petrified in stone. The child grasping for her mother's arm. The old man caught in sleep, his hands covering his eyes. The cowering young men, curled in almost fetal positions, and the old ones bent in a crouch, hiding their faces between their knees. She sees the limbs of the dead, caught by surprise, in contorted angles of pain. She imagines a burning that turns you inside out, out of yourself, out of your seared flesh.

She sees the flames, the burning, and turns away. Strolling down Via Abondanza, she walks in and out of broken houses, listening for the echoes of past lives in this deserted city. The windows of the half-shorn foundations gape like toothless mouths. Occasionally signs of life remain: the basin for the laundress, the grinding stone, the blackened loaf of bread, the water gurgling from a fountain, the spout surrounded by the mouth of a woman's chipped face, a horn of plenty still held in her frozen white arm.

And then she stops at the threshold of another small dwelling and looks down onto a mosaic floor. And there it is: wings, chips of light blue and gray mosaic, almost floating like a cloud,

drifting across the dull, darkened floor. The bird takes shape. Long spindly legs, the wings arched, ready for flight. The dark eye still staring into space. The bird, a translucent shadow, a glimpse of a crescent moon in the bright sky of day. She tries to define the color. Is it sea foam? A light blue mist, like the edge of the horizon at the sea? The color makes her breathe deeply. She doesn't know if the bird is an ibis or a crane. She imagines its slight cry in a bloodless sky.

And what remains of life? A blackened egg petrified to stone. The tilt of a wing in late afternoon light.

A Mourning Story

(In the Bar at Costa Teguise)

A cool breeze from the distant sea rustles date palm leaves as you sip your aperol spritz, your husband his martini. In this land of intense sun and a vast, cloudless sky, you are momentarily content.

Seeping into you are waves of colors: the magenta of bougainvillea, mango bursts of birds of paradise, jet-black lava rocks, glinting in the sun, leading down to a turquoise and indigo sea.
So like an abstract painting. Like the awe you felt in the room of Rothko's in DC. The blocks of orange and red that took your breath away.

Then nudging you, your husband breaks your mood—the call of the doves leading him to a bedtime story his father told him.

The mourning dove goes to sleep happy, has nightmares all night long, and wakes up to sing, to shed his grief.

You imagine the father sitting next to his child's bed, pushing curly blonde hair from his son's eyes, kissing his forehead. All to soothe an anxious boy. You know your husband has known grief—the loss of his father at 49 and later two best friends.

You too have known death that comes without warning. You believe like Chicken Little the sky could fall at any moment: a surprise diagnosis of cancer, a tumble on a patch of ice and a broken hip, a car crash. You remember the news article about a man killed in winter by an icicle that pierced his heart. Or another of the woman in Big Hill, Ky. She went blueberry picking in the brambles and stepped into a nest of rattlers. What did her children left in the car on a deserted country road, in the thick heat and dust of late summer, feel when their mother didn't return? Did they hear death rattles?

Is life always keening? Or are there songs that erase sorrow? One bird swoops down, pecks at your drink, and stares. The eye ringed in powder blue. A perfect circle.

"A moment is an eternity."

César Manrique

Sometimes the ocean is indigo and aquamarine.
Sometimes it is tinged blue grey.

Sometimes the obsidian stones glint in the sun
Sometimes they are ashen or a dull tobacco brown.

Sometimes the breeze brings cool nights
Sometimes a hot wind, a calima.

Sometimes the stones, washed by sea foam, glint in the sun.
Sometimes in this dry world they are scarred, rusted brown.

Sometimes the hills are layers of pink and terracotta.
Sometimes they are darkened by shadows of clouds.

Sometimes the white stucco houses in the distance dot the hills like wings.
Sometimes they are dwarfed by the vast sky and intense sun.

Sometimes this world of cactus, volcanic bubbles, camels, and desert
seems mummified; sometimes it is strewn with light.

I pick up a stone thrown up by the sea, mottled
by the tides. It is pocked, traces of air still caught inside.

Each moment an eternity.

A Corot Landscape

Yellow light weaves in and out
of fanned edges
of spruce poplar and locust
meadows rise in green
a thick seeping like sea grass

the only sounds
the fitful stirrings
of night breezes
and fireflies
the fitful ravaging
of children foraging for light.

ACKNOWLEDGEMENTS

Grateful acknowledgement is made to the following publications in which some of these poems first appeared:

Art Times: "Palette of Grief"
Blueline: "A Corot Landscape"
The Broadkill Review: "Io in Modern Dress"
Chantwood Magazine: "Madison, Wisconsin, 1970 (after Kent State)" and "Bess's Lament"
The Chiron Review: "This is a story about terrible itching"
Home Planet News: "Twenty-Five Years After John Lennon's Death: December 8, 2005" and "Under Siege,"
The Ghazal Page/The International Anthology of the Ghazal : "Broken Ghazal" and "Ghazal: Not All White"
Kentucky Review: "A Gift: Kentucky Nursing Home Many Years Ago"
The Shawangunk Review: "Flash Forward: On the Way to Graciosa with my Husband" and "Do you hear my words as a whisper?"
The Vassar Review: "My Young Grandparents at a Coney Island Photo Booth circa 1900"; "Wedding Relic"; "My Mother Takes Aim"; "Fade Out/Fade In"
Westchester Review: "Kentucky Hill Wife" (Featured Poem and Author's Note as well on Website)
The Write Place at the Write Time: "I am your Dutiful Daughter," "Clara Peeters Speaks: Still Lives," "Punta Mujeres: A Land of Grief," and "Vermeer's Lady Writing"

Note: Several of these poems, "The earth was still," "Going Home," "Icarus's Mother," and "Pompeii" appeared in my chapbook, *The Earth Was Still,* published by Finishing Line Press.

Several works are featured in the anthology, *An Apple in her Hand,* published by Codhill Press: "Bess's Lament," "Fade Out/Fade In," "I am your dutiful daughter," "The Leopard Housecoat," "Madison, Wisconsin,1970 (After Kent Date)," "A Moment is an Eternity," and "Punta Mujeres: Land of Grief."

Special thanks to my husband, Philip A. Schmidt, and my son, Reed Schmidt, for bringing so much light into my life.

And my deepest gratitude to family, friends, and my writing group—my trusted readers—who have supported my work over many years and have provided wise counsel and productive feedback: Marilyn Zlotnik and Peter Hultberg, Lucia Cherciu, Judy Dorney, Colleen Geraghty, Kit Goldpaugh, Eileen Howard, Tana Miller, Mary K O'Melveny, and Kappa Waugh.

A special thanks to Eric Andersen for granting permission to use lines from his song, "Thirsty Boots" in "Madison, Wisconsin, May 1970 (After Kent State).

Jan **Zlotnik Schmidt** is a SUNY Distinguished Teaching Professor at SUNY New Paltz in the Department of English where she teaches autobiography, creative writing, women's literature, American and cotemporary literature, and Holocaust Literature. She has been published in many journals including *The Cream City Review, Kansas Quarterly, The Alaska Quarterly Review, Home Planet News, Phoebe, Black Buzzard Review, The Chiron Review, Memoir(and), The Westchester Review,* and *Wind.* Her work has been nominated for the Pushcart Press Prize Series. She has had two volumes of poetry published by the Edwin Mellen Press (*We Speak in Tongues,* 1991; *She had this memory,* 2000) and two collections of autobiographical essays, *Women/Writing/Teaching (SUNY Press, 1998)* and *Wise Women: Reflections of Teachers at Mid-Life* (Routledge, *2000*). Her chapbook, *The Earth Was Still,* was published by Finishing Line Press and another, *Hieroglyphs of Father-Daughter Time,* was published by Word Temple Press. Most recently she co-edited with Laurence Carr a collection of works by Hudson Valley women writers entitled *A Slant of Light: Contemporary Women Writers of the Hudson Valley,* which won the 2013 USA Best Book Award for Anthology. Her multicultural and global literature anthology, *Legacies: Fiction, Poetry, Drama, Nonfiction,* co-authored with Dr. Lynne Crockett and the late Dr. Carley Bogarad is now in its fifth edition and used nationwide.